COPYWRITING

The Writing that Converts
People into Customers

© Copyright 2018 by Carmine Rea - All rights reserved.

The following eBook is reproduced below with the goal of providing information that is as accurate and reliable as possible. Regardless, purchasing this eBook can be seen as consent to the fact that both the publisher and the author of this book are in no way experts on the topics discussed within and that any recommendations or suggestions that are made herein are for entertainment purposes only. Professionals should be consulted as needed prior to undertaking any of the action endorsed herein.

This declaration is deemed fair and valid by both the American Bar Association and the Committee of Publishers Association and is legally binding throughout the United States.

Furthermore, the transmission, duplication, or reproduction of any of the following work including specific information will be considered an illegal act irrespective of if it is done electronically or in print. This extends to creating a secondary or tertiary copy of the work or a recorded copy and is only allowed with the express written consent from the Publisher. All additional rights reserved.

The information in the following pages is broadly considered a truthful and accurate account of facts and as such, any inattention, use, or misuse of the information in question by the reader will render any resulting actions solely under their purview. There are no scenarios in which the publisher or the original author of this work can be in any fashion deemed liable for any hardship or damages that may befall them after undertaking information described herein.

Additionally, the information in the following pages is intended only for informational purposes and should thus be thought of as universal. As befitting its nature, it is presented without assurance regarding its prolonged validity or interim quality. Trademarks that are mentioned are done without written consent and can in no way be considered an endorsement from the trademark holder.

TABLE OF CONTENTS

Introduction 1

Chapter 1: What is Copywriting? 2

Chapter 2: Copywriting Basics 5

Chapter 3: SEO Copywriting 12

Chapter 4: How to Create Your Portfolio as a Copywriter 18

Chapter 5: How Much Money can you Make Copywriting? 22

Chapter 6: Copywriting Techniques 27

Conclusion 31

INTRODUCTION

Congratulations on purchasing *Copywriting: The Writing that Converts People into Customers*, and thank you for doing so. The world of copywriting is growing increasingly chaotic. Downloading this book is the first step that you can take towards doing something about improving your writing. Such first step will not always be the easiest, which is why the information you will find in the following chapters is so important to take to heart, as they are not concepts that can be put into action immediately. If you preserve and keep these concepts in anticipation for some use in the future, you will be glad you have them on hand when that time actually comes.

The following chapters will discuss the primary preparedness principles that you will need to consider; that is, if you hope to really improve your copywriting skills and unlock the power of your writing. To achieve this end, you will want to assess the quality of your writing. This involves looking at potential issues raised by the number of words you use and how they can best be utilized to let your audience know about a particular product. It also includes various strategies you might have to carry out, to keep your audience engaged.

When you have quality already ironed out and taken care of, you will then learn everything you need to know about the different tricks to enhance your copywriting skills.

I am happy to welcome you to the world of copywriting and to help you uncover the hidden secrets of your words.

CHAPTER 1:
WHAT IS COPYWRITING?

Copywriting is the art of writing persuasive and conversion-oriented content, which requires different techniques based on the means of communication adopted.

The term, "copywriter," traces its history back in the nineteenth century. It was a label given to some journalistic editors, to indicate who was mainly responsible for drafting announcements. With the spread of mass media on a large scale, the copywriter then specialized as a real advertiser employed by advertising or communication agencies. He also worked as a freelancer who often paired up with the art director, the person who takes care of the graphics part of advertisements.

With the current state of digital marketing, copywriting activities have gone on to cover more of the many textual aspects of online content - from advertising on social media to articles for business blogs optimized from an SEO perspective. Undoubtedly, copywriting has become an essential aspect of communication on the Internet. More than knowing how to write in the specific language of reference and delivering grammatically correct texts, a copywriter is able to communicate the brand's message through words, using specific writing techniques tailored for the web.

Every day, we happen to hear and read numerous advertisements. We think of the commercials that are broadcast on radio and television, as well as the promotional pages that often fill the newspapers. This "verbal crowding" that characterizes all mass media is mainly the result of the work of a communications professional, the copywriter.

Marshall McLuhan, who is well-known for his theories on communications, also developed his own description of what a copywriter is. He defined the term in his book, "Understanding Media," showing his usual sharpness and irony. According to McLuhan, a copywriter is one who "must be like a stripper in total empathy with the immediate state of mind of his audience". Indeed, the main task of the copywriter is to write ads that capture the attention of the target audience. This brings to light an important question: what are the main rules for obtaining this result?

As often happens when creativity is involved, it is difficult to establish precise rules to serve as a manual for work. However, some fundamental guidelines can be outlined. First of all, it is essential to identify the target you want to achieve. A particular message is effective only if it adopts a language suitable for the relevant public. The more specific this is, the easier it is to get on the mark. Secondly, the form of creativity must be adapted to the content of the brief. It should be noted that the main objective is to sell, and the product must occupy a leading position with respect to the creative idea. Precisely for this reason, it is important to follow the principle of the Unique Selling Proposition, or USP, when designing an advertising or marketing strategy. This is simply the formulation of a single creative idea, which will have to stress the product feature considered the most important. Finally, the formal contradictions within an announcement must be avoided. It is crucial, for example, that the image and text say different things, so as not to have an overlap in the message being conveyed. A well-defined formal structure makes the announcement easier to decode and allows you to get in tune with the target audience more quickly.

In addition to these indications, it must be said that the work of the copywriter has evolved considerably over the last few years, especially following the widespread diffusion of the Internet. In fact, to traditional skills, we must now add a good knowledge of online writing techniques. These skills include factors such as search engine optimization (SEO); that is, writing for websites while making use of certain tricks aimed at improving the position of the site in the results provided by search engines. Therefore, it is not out of place to argue that along with the web, a new profession in the copywriting world was born, the SEO copywriter.

CHAPTER 2:
COPYWRITING BASICS

If you want to have good results online, you cannot ignore the importance of copywriting. Collectively, it is the set of all communication strategies to write in a persuasive way and to publish texts capable of moving the audience successfully.

To start, there are essential points to tackle: how to write compelling text, how to persuade your customers to buy from you, and how to effectively communicate your ideas and your proposals. First on the list are the main actions of persuasive copywriting.

Most non-professionals, when they have to sell or write to sell, tend to ignore a basic concept: you communicate to people and you need to know your target. The truth is, 90% of writers make this mistake, and all their publications will be influenced by it.

Prior to putting anything on paper, you need to adequately know the person or group of persons you are addressing. How can you write persuasive text and expect to convince someone you know nothing about? Writing without knowing the people they are addressing is a mistake many new copywriters commit.

If you have a company and create an advertisement (regardless of whether it is online or offline), you need to understand the desires of the people you are targeting. If at all possible, you have to know their wants even better than them. Thus, the first step in learning to write persuasive text is to study your audience.

Following is an illustration that will help you understand this concept, which is at the base of copywriting techniques. You are a professor and you want to sell English tutorial classes in order to earn extra money and teach this universal language. What do you do? You can probably invest in advertising by printing flyers and posters and distribute them everywhere, to inform people about the service you're offering. Since you already spent money, you expect an economic return. Unfortunately, this doesn't happen. Why? The answer is simple. You did now know the people you were addressing. Maybe you distributed the flyers to people who participated in a motorcycle fair, thinking to yourself, *"There are many people here. Surely someone will sign up for my course."*

It does not work like this. People who attend a motorcycle fair are not interested in learning English. You would have been more successful if you were distributing your flyers at the university; specifically, at the faculty of languages and among students who have been rejected by the English exam.

What you need to know about the public

You must gain a good understanding of your client. You have to know what desires you are cultivating, what fears torment him, and what drives him in a certain direction. To write an effective copy, you need to be very familiar with him. To do so, you have to answer these questions:

- What kind of person am I addressing?

- Who is he?
- How old is he?
- What does he want in life?
- What results does he want to achieve?
- What is he afraid of?
- What drives him to do what he does?
- What is that thing he wants most of all?

Create a reader persona of your ideal customer every time you create an advertisement, or write to sell an idea or to promote a product. This is the fundamental step in learning to write persuasive text. Here are 6 principles that you must always keep in mind for your copywriting techniques.

Write the benefits, not the technique

Do not talk about the technique of what you're offering, only its benefits. People do not care what features your product has, but they care about the good that it brings to their lives. List the advantages and various ways in which you will improve or facilitate customer experience.

If you really want to mention the characteristics of the product, do it for the purpose of explaining more clearly what are benefits are. Here is an example of a piece of copywriting: *"My video course lasts 200 hours but allows you to earn $ 10,000."*

Do you notice something in the above sentence? The first part states the characteristic, then the benefit. People buy your product for the benefits it can convey. Your text will be effective to the extent that you will succeed, through copywriting, to value the pluses.

When you do not know how to write persuasive text, it's helpful to remember that people buy something for what it can do, not how it is done. For instance, not everyone knows how many horses a Ferrari car has (characteristics), but everyone recognizes its speed (benefit).

You must be specific in the copy

When you talk about the advantages of your product or service, you need to be as specific as possible. Instead of saying, "*With my guitar course, you will become very good,*" indicate comprehensively what benefit your client will feel by saying, "*With my guitar course you will be able to play all the melodies you want in a short time. You can write your own songs, you will be able to seduce women to bonfires, and become the rock star of your country. Others will want to become like you.*"

It is imperative to first list the benefits a person will experience by buying what you offer. You can also give a description of its characteristics, but this is secondary. Doing the opposite is a bad idea.

If you want to learn how to write persuasive text, train yourself to enumerate, in detail, all the positive points. Make your client's experience vivid and specific.

Show everything you write

What you write becomes true in the reader's head only when you provide him with evidence to support what you are saying. Just to give a concrete and common example, travel decisions are influenced by online reviews. You will have bought a book and looked for reviews first. Have you blind-booked a hotel? No, you prefer to find out what people have been thinking about the service. The copywriter has leverage on social proof.

Before buying, you want to inform yourself if the service is good or not. When you sell your video course, your book or your product should support what you say with concrete evidence. You can use surveys from authoritative sources, reviews, tables, and charts.

If what you offer is totally new and you do not have any reviews, then you have to show significant data to show that your solution is the most suitable for your client. You should pay attention to this crucial step of always giving concrete evidence.

Create empathy by giving of "you"

The mistake you often make when copywriting is to write using "you." You have to create a familiar environment with your reader. You must use it in such a way as a long-standing friend would. When you write persuasive text, you cannot think of addressing the public as if you were a stranger.

People trust and let themselves be persuaded by those who are friendly to them. Apply this when you write on your blog, when you create a sales page, when you write a flyer, or create a brochure. Write in a simple and understandable way for your reader.

Leverage on pain and pleasure

When you work on copywriting, your purpose is to write in order to persuade or sell. To do this correctly, you have to use the two leverages of pain and pleasure.

Everything we do as human beings, we put into practice to escape from pain, which is the strongest leverage of all. This underlines the importance of knowing about your interlocutor – about learning his fears and subsequently exploiting them.

If you sell a course to effectively speak in public, what fear does your client have? It would likely be making a bad impression on stage and being judged. Having identified the weak points, you have to paint a picture: if he does not act, his fear will manifest itself.

Similar to the pain leverage you, you can also take advantage of pleasure. To do this, simply list all the benefits. Make them as detailed as possible, anticipating the pleasure you will convey to the reader. If you want to learn how to write persuasive text, capitalizing on the senses of pain and pleasure are good bases from which to start. However, you have to practice a lot.

Use deep desires in your favor

We have deep desires as human beings. Four of these correspond to points that can be exploited in copywriting techniques. We want to hear:

- Appreciated
- Important.
- Independent.
- Safer.

If you want to utilize one of these innate desires of the human being to your advantage, it is not enough for you to simply write, "*By buying this product you will feel appreciated.*" You will have to intensify the feeling of what it means to be appreciated or independent. To do this, start by answering these questions:

- What will you see when you feel appreciated and how can I describe it?
- What types of speech or words will you listen to, to you feel appreciated?

- How can I express it in detail?
- What sensations will you feel when you feel appreciated?
- How can I use words to explain it?

Once again, copywriting is not improvisation. Techniques to write persuasive text are based on the study of the field of action, and on activities that allow you to know the terrain before making a decision.

CHAPTER 3:

SEO COPYWRITING

SEO copywriting includes the techniques that allow the web writer to write texts suitable for search engines, with the purpose of securing a favorable position in the pages of Google. In order to do this, the SEO copywriter must pay attention to the use of keywords, readability, Google meta tags, and the analysis of an SEO Specialist who has conducted a keyword research.

Indeed, SEO copywriting is based on an assumption that is now clear to all - writing must be for people and not for search engines. In this way, readers will appreciate the content, and Google, in return, will provide rewards via links. This is the essence of online writing. When you work every day for the web, it seems easy to balance the text with the keywords. There are certain types of work, however, that require more attention. There are texts that need a true SEO copywriter, a person who can choose and use the most suitable words.

SEO copywriting is a job that combines online writing with search engine rules. The goal is to get quality web pages, both for people and for Google's spiders, while always having in mind the strategic objectives. It is not just about entering keywords or applying them repeatedly in the text. The same goes for the use of synonyms. In essence, SEO copywriting is balanced text.

Based on this logic, the choice and utilization of keywords have qualitative value. Would this be a good assumption? A good answer would be: SEO copywriting is the piece of a broader strategy. Through a well-defined plan, identify your goals and proceed accordingly.

Creating useful content

SEO copywriting is an attempt to climb the SERP (Search Engine Results Page) with content. This is a task for the copywriter, a person who knows the rules of search engines and online writing. For example, he understands the importance of the title tag for Google and also knows that it must be persuasive to attract a user's click.

It is not simply putting in keywords in the right places, which anyone can do. It takes much more to dominate a competitive SERP. You have to understand how to write an optimized SEO page. This involves not only pleasing Google but also the readers of the site you are writing for.

You have to work towards positioning on Google's front page. This will require you to have clear ideas and be aware of the objectives. In the foreground, it is necessary to meet the needs of those who read, using the most sought-after words. You also have to go beyond your own search intentions. Talk to the people who have commissioned the work and do not be afraid to request for information. Try to enter the mind of an average user. What are his questions? What are his needs? To accomplish this, you have to work with qualitative and quantitative data.

This is the collection work addressed in the succeeding paragraphs. At the outset, you have to maintain the perspective that writing for the web and doing SEO Copywriting basically means meeting the needs of readers. There are no black hat mysteries and secret techniques. Simply put, if a text is liked by internet users, it will gain Google's favor. The quality of the content directly meets their questions and information needs. This is the real SEO writing technique: satisfy the reader. Always. Also, improve the user's experience.

SEO Copywriting starts with a brainstorming job with colleagues, customers, and potential readers. The first two can be contacted easily; the third, on the other hand, must be intercepted through tools and common sense.

Understanding research intentions

One of the key aspects of SEO copywriting is grasping the intentions of research and then writing content to meet these. How do you put this theory into practice? You must focus on the main types of searches that people use Google for, such as these queries:

- Navigational, when the user wants to go somewhere.
- Transactional, when the user wants to do something.
- Informational, when the user searches for information.

The navigational research calls into question the name of a specific brand and is made by those who already have a precise idea about what they want. Second is the transactional kind that contemplates an action, usually a purchase intention. Finally, there is informational research, that corpus of queries that corresponds to 80% of online searches. The positioning on search engines passes through the work you do on these keywords.

Information research and blogging

Informational inquiries are those questions users ask in Google on how to do something. What does this mean for those who have to think about keywords?

The answer is in the chart that organizes the publication of content. There are pages that respond to commercial research, which is associated with the willingness to purchase. There are likewise blog articles that respond to the need for information. The one who works on keywords must comprehend what objective is hidden behind a search and offer the best answer. Blog articles have a goal, as do landing pages and e-commerce cards. Nevertheless, everyone works toward the same direction. That is the turnover.

You have to find out the research intentions in order to do a good job of SEO copywriting and to position yourself in Google. Two of the best ways you can do this is by working with online tools that give you details and figures about the searches of potential readers (what people are looking for on search engines) and following the communities where discussions are developed. In this way, you gather a lot of information. You must then come up with ways to use these results. The SEO copywriter starts from a keyword, from a precise need, and the means to optimize a page to answer a query.

As suggested by famous SEO expert, Cyrus Shepard, on the blog *Moz*, everything starts with a defined topic that must be communicated to Google. However, attention must be paid to details. Resist researching single keywords. Instead, move towards exploring your keyword themes by examining secondary keywords that are closely related. When people talk about your topic, what words do they use to describe it? What are the properties of your subject? Use these supporting keyword phrases as cast members to build content around your central theme.

You do not have to search only the main keyword, the one you will have to follow to optimize the main points of the web page. You must also focus on looking for associated words and phrases, to deepen your research intentions and create the best content.

Still, you have to be circumspect in utilizing keywords. Do you know what happens when you exaggerate with keywords? Try to guess – a penalty from Google. This is the worst possible situation for a copywriter. Readability should always be the first point.

Web copywriting: how to write online

You might ask: is there an existing set of techniques for SEO writing? Actually, the road to follow is simply to define a topic and work on it, to deepen the people's interest. The goal is not to enchant Google with magic formulas; rather, it is to create text based on research about people and the information gathered thru observation of communities. The text of the web page sees the reader in the middle and should have the following main components.

Page title

This is the H1 tag. It is the element that a viewer sees before he starts to read. To catch the reader's attention and convince him to explore further, it must be as catchy as possible. In this case, a little persuasive copy does not hurt, while also incorporating the most important keywords. This is how to write an effective headline.

SEO-friendly URL

A good URL structure, from the SEO point of view, foresees the presence of the main keywords. This is another element that is shown in the SERP and is highlighted when it matches the query.

Paragraphs of the copy

Here, you have to practice your web writing skills to be able to write great content. Comprehensive articles can answer questions related to a specific theme. Your style of writing should be simple but never banal. Avoid wandering from the subject at hand, but create connections with related topics.

Subtitles (header)

These have H2, H3, and H4 tags. Paragraph titles help people scan the text and easily find sections they want to focus on. Tags are commonly used for correlates that have a greater search volume, to meet the readers' needs on finding more interesting points.

CHAPTER 4:
HOW TO CREATE YOUR PORTFOLIO AS A COPYWRITER

It seems like a simple detail to fine-tune, but how do you create a portfolio as a copywriter? By adding a page of your blog or website, making a list of completed jobs, and entering the link in the main menu. It does not take a miracle of technique to do such a thing, does it?

Not exactly. Do the best American copywriters have a portfolio? The answer to this question is not really certain, but those who want to promote their names and find new customers online need a page like that. They cannot be content with just a list of jobs.

It does not work like this. Landing pages can make the difference because they turn a reader into a potential customer. The synthesis of the experiences and the work carried out previously can ferry interesting contacts towards your attention. A landing page represents a powerful persuasive weapon at your service.

Are you curious to find out how to create a portfolio for copywriters? Here is a recipe.

The first step to publishing a portfolio for copywriters is to create a page on your blog or website to host your work. The portfolio is nothing more than a list of the various jobs you have done in a given period of time. *WordPress* web pages are perfect for this.

Now, go to a specific section in your blog's dashboard, and proceed to create the portfolio page. Immediately after, go to the *WordPress* menu and enter your portfolio page in the main menu. In other words, this resource must be reachable right away. It must not be hidden, but immediately visible from those who arrive on the blog. Label the page as "Portfolio."

Divide the text into sections

Now that you have an existing page, how do you go about creating a copywriter's portfolio? Begin by dividing the resource into sections. Make a list of tasks and projects you have done as a copywriter and divide them by categories. That could be naming, payoffs, brochures, landing pages, websites, and more. The idea here is to isolate a single type of work and give value to everything that deserves to be listed.

Choose what you show to your customers

Not everything can and should be included in a copywriter's portfolio. This is the same principle that is applicable when creating a good resume. You to give emphasis to jobs that can attract the attention of the audience you want to reach.

At first, you may have to add a little of 'everything' if the page will remain empty otherwise.

However, with the passage of time, you have to be more selective. Readers are easily distracted and do not have the time or the want to browse long and articulate documents. You have to aim for the synthesis.

You must include work that highlights your skills as a copywriter. This page will consist of writings related to body copy, the headline of web pages and newsletters, tagline, payoff, slogans, and site pages. Do not forget to mention blogging and naming, too.

Work on visual and copy

This is the most important part since it encompasses the creation of the portfolio itself. You have to describe the work done, also adding all the elements to contextualize. That will consist of company, project, description of the activity carried out, and corresponding links for verification. If possible, enter a testimony.

Remember that all these must be clear and verifiable. People want to see someone who testifies in favor of another. Furthermore, you have to consider the visual aspect. The work of the copywriter, often and willingly, is intertwined with that of the graphic designer. Your portfolio may need to capture the screenshots of a project. Thus, you have to think about photo galleries as well.

There are several plugins that allow you to create galleries for images, along with *WordPress* themes that are also designed for this purpose. In any case, never forget to update the portfolio page, add jobs, and remove unnecessary or outdated information. Always optimize.

Use the authority of customers

In this case, you have to think about the fundamental steps of persuasion, especially those indicated by Robert Cialdini. A very useful tip is to use your portfolio to insert elements of authority. A principle that, according to *Wikipedia*, says this:

The assertions sustained by a reference to a relevant figure, real or presumed, or presented as if they were derived from that figure/institution, increase their persuasive value.

This means that in your copywriter portfolio, you are allowed to put in logos and graphic references that are identified with famous companies, especially those that your target clients would readily recognize. Think about this: with the logo of an international company or a web agency listed in your field, wouldn't your chances for getting work be better?

I do not have a project to show: how do I create the portfolio?

A challenge that many new copywriters face is creating a portfolio when they do not have any work or noteworthy tasks to show yet. This problem can be overcome with a little flexibility. For example, you can create a blog and start writing and publishing articles. It is already a good way to develop a portfolio.

For these pages, you can think about hypothetical customers and perform activities to publish on the blog as examples. Make this an avenue to showcase the way you work, your technique, and your knowledge. Of course, you have to make it clear that the customer is someone you imagined and not a real one. In the meantime, however, your portfolio is already taking shape.

CHAPTER 5:
HOW MUCH MONEY CAN YOU MAKE COPYWRITING?

The rate card for a copywriter should be a document that is able to solve the great anguish of those who work in the field of writing, which is: how much do I have to ask for my work? Defining the price is a real issue and an obstacle that needs to be overcome by those who start operating in this sector.

Just as it is very difficult to put a price tag on creative work, there is likewise no clear parameter to delineate a copywriter's rate card. For many, this is dramatic news. Everything would be easier with, perhaps, an hourly regulation to give your pen a way to follow. Some of the most common questions asked are: Do I ask too much or too little? Will I look like an amateur if I keep my rates low? Or an inflated balloon if too high? Coming up with standard rates would be a great thing, but the simple truth is that it is impossible to draw up such a table. This is due to a number of reasons.

The rate card is a powerful document because it solves doubts and exonerates you from reflecting and revolutionizing your needs every day. You do not have to customize each quote. You only have to look at the price list and give the price of your work. This is why the fee for a copy could be a resource.

All these become even more difficult when you work in ghostwriting, which involves working in the background, so you do not have a clear comparison with the world around you. The personal branding experts, though, have this clear advice: work for free or ask a lot. Do not compromise. Never be satisfied with crumbs. However, when you do not have the tools to define a starting point, look for the security, the scheme, and the stability of a rate card. The only problem is that the rate card does not actually exist. Do you know why? And do you know how much a freelance copywriter earns?

According to the Antitrust Authority, the rate card is illegal.

This is the primary reason why it is extremely difficult to have a single and common copywriting card. This writer was unaware of this particular detail until James Fitch, an important copywriter, shared a document that enshrined such passage.

Technically, creating a shared copywriter rate card is not a legal transaction, since it can be classified as an agreement restrictive of competition (a behavior that by definition falls within the illicit). Since advertising is not an ordinary profession, there is the possibility of enjoying minimum rates.

In 2009, the defunct TP Association published jointly with the ACPI, a guide that had exactly the purpose of providing references, albeit in the form of indicative price ranges, with regard to the rates to be formulated in the estimate. The initiative was promptly challenged and blocked by the Antitrust Authority, which, in 2012, condemned the two associations to a symbolic fine, distrusting them from reiterating the initiative. It should be noted that the boundaries of the question are particularly labile. On a purely theoretical level, even discussing informally among colleagues within a Facebook group of professionals sharing their own tariff references could configure a behavior aimed at limiting free competition, since it would lay the foundations for a potential agreement between more professionals among their competitors.

As you can well understand from the above words, there is no legal possibility to create an official copywriter rate card. But this is only the first reason that closes the doors to this need.

Creativity has no hourly rate

This is the second point that makes it impossible to create a rate card. Creative work cannot be summarized, nor can it be enclosed in an hourly rate for copywriters who have to write 1,000 words per hour to earn the minimum wage. It does not work this way.

A copywriter cannot be paid for a number of beats or based on the time needed to attend to a customer. The reason is simple. There are jobs that require a few words and can be closed in a short time but highlight your creativity and experience.

A good illustration would be the creation of a slogan and subsequently evaluating it. This can be done in 30 minutes or 2 days. What parameters will then be used as the basis for payment? For a few words, will the price be only 50 cents? The work is too varied to create a good estimate.

Different valuations of work

Another reason to close the door to a shared copywriter rate card is the value given to work. Such value is not linear, and you cannot expect everyone to align with your way of seeing the world.

For instance, you see an item as worth 40 dollars and ask for this price. Another may think that it is worth more and will give a different value. The same goes for a product or brand names, a landing page, or an email object. Everyone can give the value they prefer to their work. This is a free market and this is the life that the freelance copywriter must contend with.

How to create a private rate card

While it may not be possible to create an hourly rate for copywriters, it is also true that a professional must start in some way. Therefore, it is suggested that you create your own personal scheme with a list of services. Take a paper and a pen, and using a mind map or some other tool, start defining all the activities you do like naming, making slogans, creating headlines, writing blog posts and press releases, etc.

Give a corresponding minimum price to these items. It is you who must decide this. Others cannot choose the worth of the work you do. Remember, however, that experience has value and must be paid. You cannot define the price based on time or number of measures. There are some elements, though, that can determine a higher price for the estimate. For example:

- Fast delivery.
- Particularly complex topics.
- SEO copywriting work for testing a blog/site.
- Editing and writing on paper.

Your price calculations must take into account the taxes related to the VAT number and the expenses of your business. If you have an agency, for example, you must include rent, telephone, company electricity consumption, and the cost of an employee. In short, the right price is the highest price you can propose. This is why personal branding becomes essential. This enables you to communicate your value to customers.

How much does a copywriter earn?

How much does an advertising copywriter earn? You can be a copywriter with a high salary. On the other hand, you can also work freelance and obtain an important quote. The real scenario in America, however, is that the work of a copywriter is not the highest paid. Rather, you must have an important brand to raise prices.

Being a copywriter and earning more money is not child's play. Monetizing in this field means making a name for yourself. In the beginning, you have to agree to work for a few dollars, but as soon as you can create a good portfolio, you have a few more possibilities. This is especially true if you can combine the needs of creative writing with SEO copywriting.

An important concept that is worth reiterating is that it is not possible to create a rate card for a copywriter for different reasons. The first concerns a legal question, the second is related to the practice of price, and the third is due to differences in personal parameters. Creative work is difficult to schematize in a price list.

What you can do is simply define a list of activities that you perform and indicate a starting point. You can then progressively update the prices based on your circumstances.

CHAPTER 6:

COPYWRITING TECHNIQUES

The power of words can change a company's future. This might be a strong claim, but after reading this chapter, you will understand the reason for this statement. It is the use of effective copywriting techniques that offer value to customers.

Speaking from personal experience, this writer asserts that having a love for words is crucial to copywriting. Continuing education and experience can play their part, but when it comes to copywriting, it would not be possible to satisfy a client without it.

Start right away by telling yourself that in order to create value with words, you need to use effective copywriting techniques. These are full of a talking and connected language in which, along with the application of an SEO strategy, you get carried away by the rhythm of the sentences, the light and non-resonant sounds, breathing between commas and periods, all capable of giving effect to a thought.

The skill of mixing all these elements together is not easy to acquire at all. Writing may be for everyone, but doing it to achieve a goal is one of the most difficult aspects of the big and complex world of content marketing. Many vital ingredients need to be present to achieve results through copywriting techniques:

- choose a strategy suited to the target;
- evaluate the right tools to communicate;
- organize useful resources for what is told;
- consider the client as a person, and not as a public.

To all these components, add the most important: the ability to tell by revealing one's own character. Only a company that offers its client something of himself can be appreciated. The customer wants to feel pampered and not deceived by the phrases made (what do you think when you read "industry leader"?). He wants to find out who is behind a brand, to feel part of something beautiful, because it is clean from logic oriented exclusively to the business. Further, the customer wants to bring stories home. It is not because he loves storytelling. Most often than not, he might not be even aware of what it is. He wants to know the stories because they transform a product or a service into something useful and indispensable.

Presenting a company with copywriting techniques

It is clear that in order to make a company known, it is necessary to choose the right words – words that talk about the business not with the objective of selling but offering added value instead. To accomplish this effectively, copywriting techniques are a big help. These are the tricks that word professionals use to mix strategy and heart together.

How do you do it concretely?

Before the indispensable techniques to show the corporate soul of a brand will be discussed, there is something you must do beforehand.

Approach the screen.

Do not worry, you will only be told to scan each syllable well.

Before writing about a company, listen to what the entrepreneur has to say.

Do not think about the right words. For now, lay aside the thought that you need to put into practice everything you have learned about SEO copywriting. Forget the company's strategies for a moment. Take some time to listen to what the brand wants to tell you.

Translate his message and read what is inside his entrepreneurial heart. Live with the entrepreneur the emotions, and the features that make what he sells unique.

Listen to it several times, take a long breath and put everything in your mind.

Here and now, you are ready to write using copywriting techniques. Now, you can choose the right words. Five essential techniques are suggested:

1. Define a tone of voice that will speak for the company.
2. Capture your attention with an appealing incipit that contains the main keyword of your SEO strategy.
3. It takes care of the simplification and the legibility of the text.
4. Create a link with the reader through words.
5. Share a true story.

The copywriting explained to the client is how important it is to tell oneself online. If you follow this path, it becomes the best way to empathize with the customer who does not need a showcase site that displays a list of products and services. He wants to know and satisfy all his consumer curiosity, to understand, and imagine with his mind. All these are possible, thanks to words.

Company and reader become two characters of a common journey, in which one esteems the other.

A company or an entrepreneur who is presenting and offering himself online should do so without fear and doubt. He must not be afraid of making mistakes. In the event this happens, he admits the mistake and prepares to make improvements. A company grows in small steps together with the words it publishes. It does not insist on being seen for what it is not. It does not self-criticize, nor does it promise the impossible. In addition, it listens to the advice of those who follow its adventures on the web, those who show themselves to be human. If all these are allowed to happen, between a web marketing strategy and an essential dose of empathy with the customer, words can create value and lead to a result. This is how the fate of a company will change.

CONCLUSION

Thank you for making it through to the end of *Copywriting: The Writing that Converts People into Customers!* Let's hope it was informative and able to provide you with all the tools you need to achieve your goals, whatever they may be. Just because you've finished going over this book doesn't mean there is nothing left to learn on the topic. Expanding your horizons is the only way to find the mastery you seek.

The next step is to stop reading and to start doing whatever it is that you need to do in order to ensure that you are able to develop an amazing copy. If you find that you still need help in getting started, you will likely have better results by creating a schedule that you hope to follow. This can include strict deadlines for various parts of the tasks, as well as the overall completion of your preparations.

Studies show that complex tasks that are broken down into individual pieces, together with corresponding deadlines, have a much greater chance of being completed when compared to something that has a general need of being completed, but no real timetable for doing so. Even if it seems silly, go ahead and set your own deadlines for completion, along with indicators of success and failure. After you have successfully done the required preparations, you will be glad you did. For example, you can think about practicing one new copywriting trick every day before becoming a general master of the power of your words. It is your choice, and it is the beauty of mastering your writing ability.

Once you have tried the same exercises many times, it is the right moment to invite your friends and ask them to try the same tricks. They are going the techniques, and best of all, see incredible results.

Finally, if you found this book useful in any way, a review on Amazon is always appreciated!

DESCRIPTION

Let's not mince words here: most business writing is tedious, pompous and bereft of the tiniest sliver of personality. It's nearly impossible for customers to cut through the "innovative solutions" and "passion for customer service," and find out who can *actually* give them what they need.

For the business owner who's willing to do something different, though, it represents a major and inexpensive competitive advantage.

This book lays out the basic simple principles that allow business owners, even those with no writing experience, to attract and enchant their dream customers. With clear and concise explanations of what works and why, besides examples of the best and worst text out there, you'll have all the necessary tools to turn readers into buyers into raving fans. Give your writing skills an instant upgrade

In this short book, you'll learn:

- Simple techniques to turn your dull-as-dishwater business marketing into "can't resist" copy even if you don't think of yourself as a "good writer."
- How to make price irrelevant and be the *only* choice for your ideal customer by changing nothing except your copywriting.
- The business writing "rules" you should revel in breaking.
- Why copying your competitors is a dangerous waste of time, and what to do instead (without spending hours searching for ideas).

- The easily avoidable mistakes that are turning your customers off even if they don't know it.
- How to "read your customers' minds," and get them looking for reasons to buy from you.
- **And much more...**

www.ingramcontent.com/pod-product-compliance
Lightning Source LLC
Chambersburg PA
CBHW031557210526
45464CB00003B/1322